A Guide to Collaboration

Working Models of Comprehensive Community Projects

by Bill Locke and Joel Christie, PhD

AuthorHouse™
1663 Liberty Drive
Bloomington, IN 47403
www.authorhouse.com
Phone: 1-800-839-8640

Published by AuthorHouse   05/18/2012

ISBN: 978-1-4772-0853-3 (sc)
ISBN: 978-1-4772-0854-0 (e)

Library of Congress Control Number: 2012908962

Any people depicted in stock imagery provided by Thinkstock are models, and such images are being used for illustrative purposes only.
Certain stock imagery © Thinkstock.

This book is printed on acid-free paper.

Because of the dynamic nature of the Internet, any web addresses or links contained in this book may have changed since publication and may no longer be valid. The views expressed in this work are solely those of the author and do not necessarily reflect the views of the publisher, and the publisher hereby disclaims any responsibility for them.

Executive Summary

There is a time when worlds must come together for the greater good. That is the time when a community decides to undertake a project that is bigger than the mandate of any one organization. Such a Comprehensive Community Project (CCP) requires a partnership involving key stakeholders who will direct and govern the CCP. As such, they must provide direction, monitoring, support and accountability, in order to develop, implement and keep the project on track. They must also champion the project, ensure that it has the resources it needs, and link the project to a wide network with high-level influence.

That partnership engages complementary organizations in the fulfillment of a common vision and mission. A CCP is too large and complex to be conducted by any one party alone, or by a diverse set of parties working separately – or worse, in competition with one another. Working together, they can share strengths, leverage resources and multiply their efforts.

If the leader of an organization sits as a Director on the Governing Unit of the partnership, he or she must be prepared to act in the best interests of the Partnership while in that role, even if it involves some sacrifice to some aspect of his or her organization in order to achieve the greater good and realize the vision of the Partnership.

Most successful partnerships have a full-time CCP Manager, who acts much like an Executive Officer in conjunction with the Governing Unit to oversee the CCP. Otherwise, the project will flounder with each of the stakeholders attempting to run the CCP from the side of their desks while devoting most of their time and energy to running their own organizations.

There are many kinds of structures of partnerships, and many ways for partnering organizations to govern and join forces.

The most effective partnership structures are as follows:

1. <u>Coalitions</u>, which have strong partners, strategic synergies, complementary roles and commonly agreed upon decision-making and accountability processes.
2. <u>Constellations</u>, which are driven by local communities. This model draws upon a common vision but is led by local groups focused on local results.
3. <u>Franchises</u>, which agree to a very detailed business, program and service delivery plan with clear roles, responsibilities, tasks and accountability measures for each "franchise", like MacDonald's International with many similar restaurants.
4. <u>Conglomerates</u>, in which stakeholders keep their autonomy; a common vision and decision-making process cements their efforts.

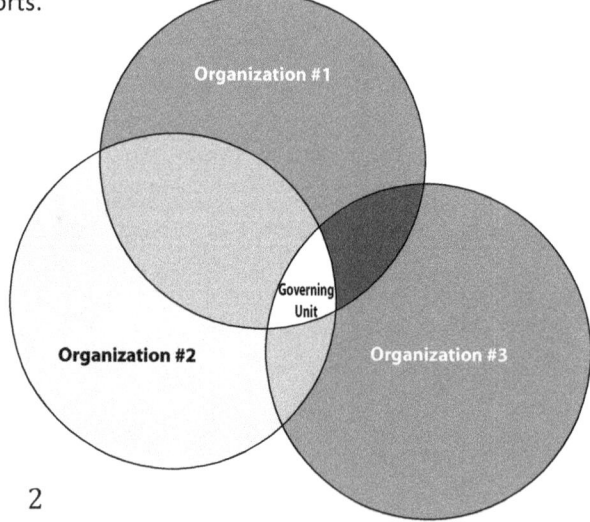

Within any given structure, the degree to which a given organization chooses to join with the others can be represented on a Coalescence Spectrum. This scale shows six levels of autonomy with its associated degree of interdependence.

Level of Coalescence

High level of autonomy for each organization; less joint decision-making

Low level of autonomy for each organization; more interdependence and joint decision-making

1. **Network**: loosely defined body which shares information
2. **Alliance**: joining forces on certain aspects of projects, such as marketing or fundraising
3. **Coordinating Council:** central decision-making, sharing of resources and clearly defined roles and budget
4. **Collective**: formalized partnership with shared leadership and decision-making
5. **Collaboration**: linked arms between partners, high trust and extensive communication
6. **Operating Council**: meshing of operations, programs and resources with a common structure and decision-making process

A clearly defined understanding of the partnership, its goals and objectives, roles and responsibilities, outcomes, milestones, decision-making processes and evaluation methods greatly helps in setting the course for action for every stakeholder. One of the most useful tools for a CCP is a 'Roadmap', outlining each key step and the expectations for Executives, Middle Management, Supervisors and Frontline Workers from all of the partnering organizations.

The Comprehensive Community Project is based on the assumption that none of us is as smart or capable as all of us. No one party has the mandate, resources or ability to address a nationwide or regional challenge. The synergy among organizations is required to truly achieve the ends of the CCP.

Table of Contents

A Joint Vision for the Future

Large-scale social change requires broad cross-sector coordination. Often organizations have their own grand visions and missions. At times, individual organizations cannot accomplish these great goals by themselves. They require an all-encompassing approach in which a group of stakeholders join forces to address a specific social issue. That Comprehensive Community Project forge efforts in a clearly defined way for the common good.

Comprehensive Community Project (CCP)

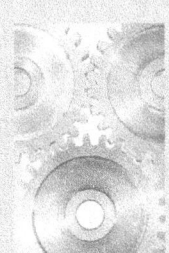

A Comprehensive Community Project contextualizes the vision for that community, region or nation. It takes the vision and applies it to a community's realities, grappling with the overarching trends. For example, it identifies and takes into consideration all of the key drivers that will impact that vision. This could include demographic trends, religious affiliations, national cultures, education levels, government policies or economic trends that need to be considered in the development of the plan.

Inter-Organizational Development

A Comprehensive Community Project requires that stakeholder organizations work together and in conjunction with the community to make the CCP reality at a local, regional or national level. They must somehow coalesce by agreeing on how they will work together over time. An inter-organizational structure or partnership is required to oversee, implement and sustain the CCP. This can involve varying levels of coalescence.

Community Development

Once the CCP is completely planned and commitments are made, organizations can work together to address local issues and needs. This allows organizations to determine how each can achieve common ends at the community level. The high-level vision of the CCP must be seen from the view of local citizens and how it will meet their local needs. Together, the local citizens will incorporate the Dream into their everyday lives.

Rationale for this Guide

What is the need for this guide? What is it designed to accomplish? We hope that it will identify common hurdles, pitfalls, and challenges related to partnership and provide means to address them. It is thereby designed to clarify and simplify what is normally a very complex exercise of uniting stakeholders' efforts to develop and carry out a CCP.

CCP's are intended to pull things together – to amalgamate efforts and create synergy. Rather than a diverse set of many small projects with diverse stakeholders working independently (and in some cases in competition), CCP's are designed to unite stakeholders so that they will work toward strategic alignment of vision, mission, goals, objectives, resources, outputs and outcomes.

This is the challenge: many times, leaders find it very difficult to govern, manage and provide healthy processes at a national level in a win-win fashion. When partnering organizations have different organizational cultures, values, languages, personalities, and agendas, it can create a *win-lose* situation with diverging agendas, misalignments and conflict.

How can diverse organizations come together so they can develop and implement a CCP successfully? What are some of the most effective ways to bring cohesion - united structure, joint management and uniting processes? This guide aims to provide tips and techniques related to governance, including structures, strategies and processes in the context of CCP's.

Governing

Governance - What is it?

According to David Renz (An Overview of Nonprofit Governance, 2004), governance is "a *process* of providing strategic leadership by setting direction, making policy and strategy decisions, overseeing and monitoring organizational performance and ensuring overall accountability." This process determines how authority is exercised, how decisions are made, how stakeholders have their say, and how decision-makers are held accountable. [1]

CCP's require organizations to join forces in many areas, including governance of their joint effort. It must also be rooted in each of the communities or neighborhoods to be impacted by the initiative.

Roles of a Governing Unit

A Governing Unit stands between the outside world and the operations of the Partnership; it gives direction to the overall efforts and ensures that the beneficiaries' interests are met. It is externally focused. It flies high, like an eagle, and looks out to the horizon. It is also internally focused, setting policy, monitoring and supporting action and ensuring accountability. Like an eagle, it has sharp eyesight, drawing upon and examining details as needed.

The Governing Unit has four key roles:

1. **Governor**: This role is internally focused. It has four key characteristics:
   a. Accountability: Organizations must have someone to answer to, who will hold everyone to agreed-upon outcomes..
   b. Transparency: Honesty and authenticity pave the way for reliable and relevant information about finance, programs and services, and the management of resources.
   c. Predictability: This ensues from clear guidelines, regulations and role definitions that are fair, uniformly enforced and known in advance.
   d. Participation: Engagement allows the Governing Unit to obtain reliable information, serves as a reality-check and watchdog, and provides feedback by users of services.

Governing Units also have three key externally oriented roles: Champion, Resource Provider and Networker. These roles connect the organization to the outside world. A successful Governing Unit is pro-active, while uniformly representing and acting on behalf of the organization and its initiatives in accordance with agreed-upon protocols and policies:

2. Champion: The Governing Unit is in a unique position to advocate on behalf of the organization and its cause to the external community, potential stakeholders and partners. Members of the Governing Unit also must serve as ambassadors to the outside world.

3. Resource Provider: The champion role spills over into advocacy with stakeholders such as funders and other resource partners. Where the Governing Unit members have resources or can bring resources from their respective organizations, the Governing Unit can also provide resources directly. Conflict of interest must be uppermost in the minds of Governing Unit members to ensure they are acting in the best interests of this organization and this cause, rather than their self-interests or the interests of another organization that they represent.

4. Networker: It is in the best interests of an organization to include Governing Unit members with influence and a wide network of high-level relationships. A business example: a Governing Unit member sitting on the national President's Club, which consists of captains from industry, and which opens up doors in the corporate sector.

A New Mindset: Comprehensive Community Project

A new project, which accomplishes more than any one partner alone could accomplish, requires a new mindset. That mindset values the different strengths of each of the participating organizations, looks at a united effort, and focuses on synergies. It sees 1+1=3. This new way of thinking is essential to the implementation of the CCP.

The Governing Unit owns and oversees the CCP. The Directors of the Governing Unit are responsible for the success or failure of each of the components of the Comprehensive Community Project. No one Director or organization owns the entire CCP. The CCP is owned by all of the participating organizations embodied in the Governing Unit.

The Partnership consists of a number of organizations which each have elements in the Partnership and elements outside, including their mandate, programs and services, allocation of resources, and decision-making. Organizations participating in the Partnership have overlapping mandates and actions:

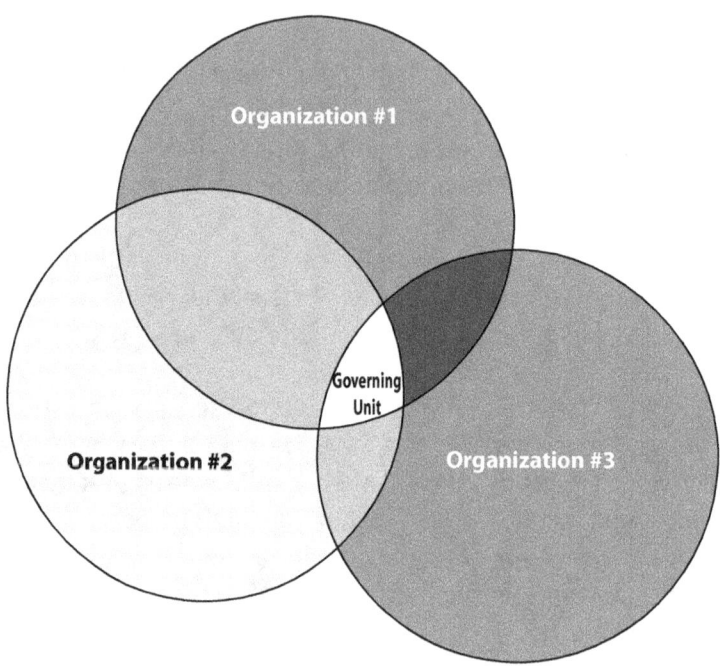

This means that the Directors of the Governing Unit are members of both the Partnership and their own organization. Each Director of the Partnership must act in the best interests of the Partnership and the fulfillment of the Comprehensive Plan. This may require that a Director "wear different hats" at different times. He or she must be able to wear the hat of Director while at the table of the Governing Unit, then take that hat off and put on the hat of Leader of his or her organization when away from the table, and negotiate between them.

What is It?

Within this context, partnership is "the active relationship of stakeholder organizations working together towards the fulfillment of a common set of goals." In this case, the goal is to govern, plan, perform, monitor and sustain a CCP. Partnerships can take many different forms.

Why Partner?

Partnership, when performed effectively, brings win-win situations for all parties[3]. Partnership allows participants to share and leverage:

- **Resources**: Practical knowledge and tangible assets
- **Skills**: Specialized abilities
- **Connections**: Networks and influence

It offers its partners:
- **Diversification** of skills, talents, capabilities and expertise
- **New perspectives**: A chance to meet with and learn from diverse groups and gain an improved understanding of the community.
- **Reduction in duplication:** The opportunity to reduce overlap in services offered
- **Increased synergies:** multiplication of resources
- **Additional contacts:** trusted relationships with people of influence, knowledge and resources
- **Comprehensive approach:** The ability to conduct more extensive service from beginning to end

Potential Challenges with Partnerships
- Organization mission drift
- Loss of control
- Complex communications and decision-making
- Conflicts between the interests of the Partnership and that of individual organizations
- Drawing down of already limited organization resources including time and money

Possible Roles of Partners:
- Sharing specialized skills (e.g. networking, marketing, planning)
- Sharing ideas and perspectives to address complex issues
- Coordinating services and initiatives
- Making services more readily available to clients
- Providing volunteers
- Donating space or equipment
- Funding or fundraising

It is absolutely essential to define the terms of partnership clearly at the beginning of the relationship.
This includes the nature of the relationship itself. Are you embarking on a network, cooperative, partnership, collaborative or integrative relationship? Will each partner have the same degree of closeness within the chosen structure? Keep in mind that definitions of these terms vary widely throughout the current literature on the subject. At the beginning of the partnership, locate the ideal intensity of the partnership on the spectrum and give working definitions of commonly used terms specific to this partnership at hand. A formal Memo of Understanding (MOU), which articulates the Terms of Reference among all of the partnering organizations and recognizes their own unique contribution, goes a long way to setting up a healthy relationship at the outset.

Be sure to carefully consider whether your organization is ready to collaborate.
- Do you have a clearly defined vision and purpose in mind for the collaborative effort?
- Are you willing to make a firm commitment?
- Do you have adequate time and funding?
- Would changes and new ideas be welcomed or resisted?
- Is the proposed partner a good fit with your organization?

Key success factors in collaboration include:
- Mutual respect, understanding and trust
- Members all see the collaboration is in their self-interest
- Ability to compromise
- Development of clear roles and policy guidelines
- Open and frequent communication
- Shared vision
- Skilled leadership

Conflict should not necessarily be avoided as it can be indicative of much-needed change and difficult issues being brought to the forefront. When serious conflicts arise, consider recruiting a neutral third-party mediator.

Partnership Structure

A Partnership Structure provides the "container" for organizations to work together in fulfillment of the CCP. It houses the Governing Unit, aligns the organizations and defines the processes for making the Dream a reality. The Partnership requires a Governing Unit to oversee the initiative in the country or region and to define the CCP. The Governing Unit provides governance, which involves the exercise of authority, direction and control of a CCP in order to ensure that its purpose is achieved.[3]

A Partnership combines the forces of a number of stakeholders for a common end that they separately cannot achieve as effectively as working together. A Partnership for such ambitious ends must fuse the efforts of people, organizations and entire communities.

Partnership Structure: Means and Process

Rather than presenting structure as an end unto itself, this guide demonstrates the use of structure to fulfill the functions of the joint effort. It provides a means to work together interdependently to meet the objectives of the CCP.

Full-Time CCP Manager Role

For the Partnership to be successful, it needs a full-time person in charge who reports to the Partnership Governing Unit, and who is responsible for managing the day-to-day operations of the Partnership. Leaders who participate in such Governing Units are simply too busy to fulfill the extensive needs of a Governing Unit and the implementation of a Comprehensive Plan without the support of a person solely committed to its ends. The CCP Manager should not report to one organization of the Partnership but to the Governing Unit of the Partnership. He or she oversees the day-to-day operation of the project, and reports on its progress, successes and challenges. His or her salary is paid out of the CCP budget although one of the participating organizations may be the fiscal agent for the CCP.

The CCP Project Manager fulfills many functions, and he or she cultivates the new mindset of the Partnership through the CCP. He or she holds together and liaises between the Governing Unit and the partnering organizations, and facilitates the meeting of milestones in the Implementation Plan:
- Administrative support (day-to-day coordination among partnering organizations related to governance):
  - Coordinating the taking and distribution of Minutes
  - Following up on action items of Minutes
  - Preparing agenda
  - Addressing concerns of Governing Unit members
- Communication between Governing Unit members and among partnering organizations and to external stakeholders (e.g. government, church bodies)
- Manager
  - Monitoring and support of operations, programs and services implemented through the stakeholder organizations
  - Outcomes: Accountability around meeting of milestones
  - Fiscal management: overseeing spending and reporting
  - Etc.

Whereas the Governing Unit oversees the direction and "glues" the various organizations together for the purpose of carrying out the CCP by bringing accountability to the Comprehensive Community Plan and to its funders, the Project Manager is the facilitator for the Partnership to help bind the Governing Unit members and other stakeholders around their common vision, mission and implementation of the CCP.

The Importance of Process: Strategies and Methods

As stated above, governance is "a *process* of providing strategic leadership by setting direction, making policy and strategy decisions, overseeing and monitoring organizational performance and ensuring overall accountability."[2]

Stage-by-Stage Process

We recommend that stakeholders come together – or "gel" – in a stage-by-stage yet iterative process. It is also contingent upon funding and other resources coming together to accomplish each stage. It may appear messy at different stages, especially the *Storming* stage:

- Stage One: *Forming*: Coming together and solidifying the group with all relevant stakeholders.
- Stage Two: *Norming*: Setting the rules of engagement, including reporting mechanisms across the organizations.
- Stage Three: *Storming*: Hashing out the plan, piloting the collaborative project in one focus area e.g. service delivery. Testing of the approach.
- Stage Four: *Equipping*: Providing and training each organization with the right people and skills, facilities and equipment to perform.
- Stage Five: *Performing*: Continuous improvement cycle: evaluation and implementation.

Discovery Process – Discernment

For the stakeholders to know and understand their position on key questions, they must take sufficient time to stand back in a somewhat detached fashion. They must discern not only the overall purpose of the CCP, but also *their* roles in it.   It involves a certain "dialing down" to see and hear and feel what is right and how to go ahead.

How does the group discern and know its way forward? It is a reflective process, which requires integrity, honesty and an attentive heart and open mind. Together, a group patiently develops a consensus around common vision, values and way forward.

This process is not something that any one person can control. Instead, it requires step-by-step group decision-making, which involves some "letting go" of individual agendas.

It is a path of discovery for individuals and the group as a whole. Discovery is a cyclical process in real life – not sequential. It has been described as a series of "Eureka moments" when everything falls into place, clarifying and defining where you are and where you and the group need to go next. This results in a clearer plan for the next phase.

There are a number of useful processes for facilitating discernment. For example, the Governing Unit can ask itself these questions:
1. *What is the spirit of the partnership - between people, team-members and units?*
2. *How do people relate to each other?*
3. *What kind of body language is used in meetings between leadership and frontlines? How do the leaders treat each other?*
4. *How do the frontline employees treat each other?*
5. *How do stakeholders outside of the organization feel about it?*

12

Based on what the group has identified in the discernment and visioning process, it must select a structure that sets out methods of decision-making and program delivery. These are the four main models. The group must choose the model that best fits their situation and adapt it, using ingredients from other models to create a management process and structure that is tailored to their particular needs.

1. Coordinated Work Model

a. **With numerous equal partners and a distribution of the work based on the strengths of each organization coordinated by the CCP Manager**

- *Governing unit – Coordinating Council or Collective or Collaboration*
- *Clearly defined partnership in the Governing Unit*
- *Common vision, values and problem-definition*
- *Commonly agreed upon decision-making and accountability processes*
- *The organizations, though separate, acts as if they are one on the CCP*
- *Each organization continues to carry out the rest of its mandate separately*
- *Complementary roles (each party has unique strengths and resources that complement the others). Functions are handled by the organization or organizations best suited to each function. For example, the organization most competent to perform education handles education. Whereas, another organization which is strongest at marketing or distribution would handle those functions.*
- *Synergies are encouraged at all levels of the organizations*

b. **Led by one or two dominant stakeholders.** This type of Partnership embeds the power and authority in one or two major stakeholders who make most of the key decisions and provide the vast majority of the resources to implement the plan. Nevertheless, these one or two stakeholders depend upon other partners to fulfill the Comprehensive Community Project.
- *Strong leadership by all partners at governance level*
- *Common vision, values and problem-definition*
- *Both partners are investing heavily in the project - more so than the other partnering stakeholders*
- *Commonly agreed upon decision-making and accountability processes*
- *Complementary roles (each party has unique strengths and resources that complement each other)*
- *Synergies are encouraged at all levels of the organizations*
- *Delegate functions to the party that is best suited to deliver them*

This is an example of a CCP focused on communications.

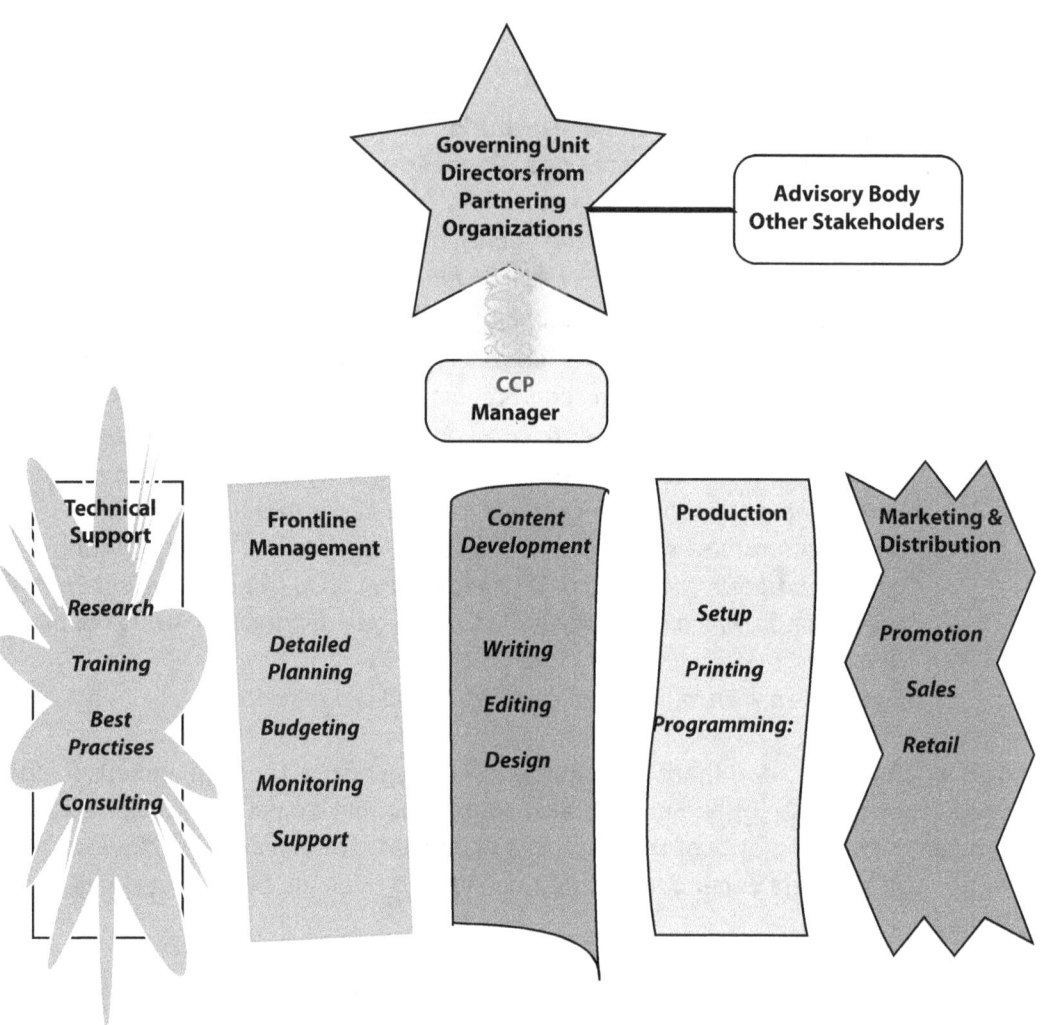

2. Constellation Model Driven by Local Communities

The Constellation model of partnering brings together groups from multiple sectors to work toward a joint outcome. The focus is on action. This model emphasizes the role of small self-organizing action teams of partners working together on a particular task or issue.

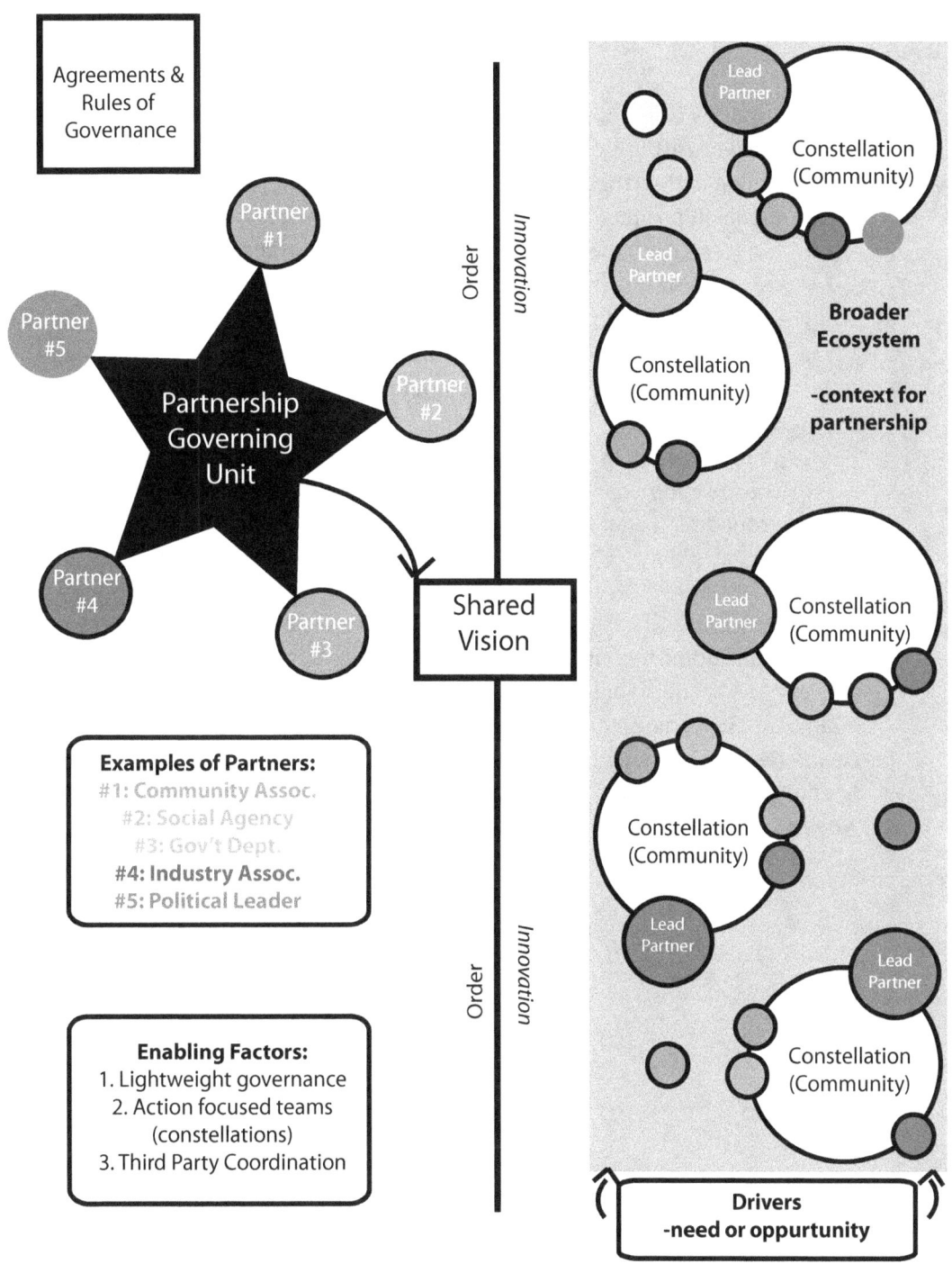

Agreements & Rules of Governance

Partner #1

Partner #5

Partner #2

Partnership Governing Unit

Partner #4

Partner #3

Order · Innovation

Shared Vision

Examples of Partners:
#1: Community Assoc.
#2: Social Agency
#3: Gov't Dept.
#4: Industry Assoc.
#5: Political Leader

Order · Innovation

Enabling Factors:
1. Lightweight governance
2. Action focused teams (constellations)
3. Third Party Coordination

Lead Partner

Constellation (Community)

Broader Ecosystem

-context for partnership

Lead Partner

Constellation (Community)

Lead Partner

Constellation (Community)

Constellation (Community)

Lead Partner

Lead Partner

Constellation (Community)

Drivers
-need or oppurtunity

15

These constellations are outwardly focused on public awareness or the broader policy environment rather than on the partnership itself.

- serious effort goes into core partnership governance and management and decision-making authority; resources are concentrated in the constellations which drive and define the partnership
- leadership rotates fluidly among partners with each partner having the chance to a) lead a constellation that matches its profiles and skills, b) participate, or c) opt out
- this emphasis on action teams accommodates the tensions around priorities that naturally exist when several groups come together
- constellations flow from opportunities, not from a rigid strategic plan. This makes it possible to balance the interests and needs of each group within the broader goal of collaboration
- this model works best when local communities are driving the implementation of the Comprehensive Community Project. It is a grassroots or bottom-up approach grounded in community based interests and needs.

3. Franchise Model

In this model, the Governing Unit is the 'Franchisor'. It defines on paper all aspects of the program, including the vision, mission, strategic plan, work plan, resources, program delivery and accountability mechanisms. Like a MacDonald's Restaurants International board, the Governing Unit ensures that every aspect and action of a local operation is clearly defined so that a local operator or "franchisee" has the resources and formula needed and can replicate the program in its own community without having to 'reinvent the wheel.'

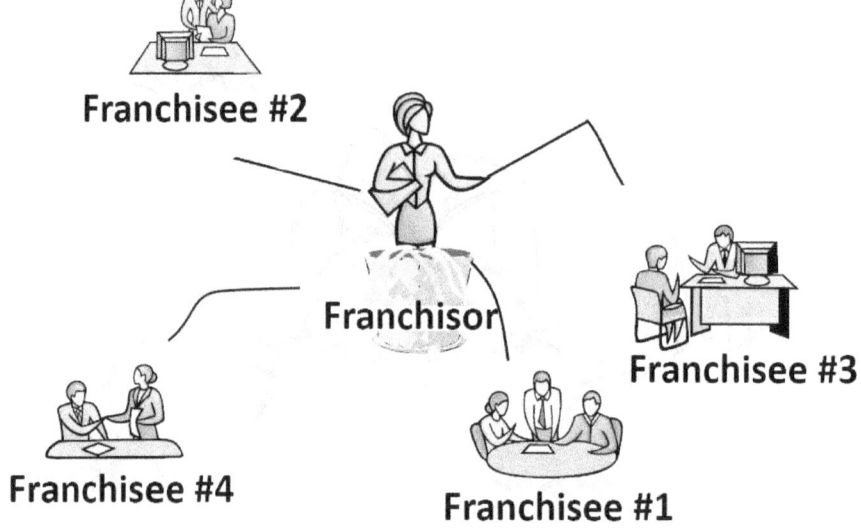

16

The Ties that Bind[6]

The ties that bind the Franchisor to the Franchisee is like a rope with five strands: Vision and Values, Accountabilities, Resource Flows, Information Systems and Rewards:

- Vision and values: The Partnership defines the overall vision, values and philosophies that shape the basic do's and don'ts. The Franchisee – the stakeholder in the community – is free to adapt, knowing that they have the support of the Governing Unit. This creates space for the parties to self-organize activities autonomously yet in an integrated way. They know when they are working within agreed upon parameters and when they are stepping outside. The offshoots remain autonomous yet connected
- Accountabilities: The responsibilities of both sides are clearly defined to ensure that all parties' interests are met, and that the Franchisee knows exactly what they are to deliver and how it will be assessed. This helps to clarify the parameters and general expectations and how they must be met. For example, funders want to know how the money was spent and the impact of the CCP.
- Resource Flows: Reliable funding, training and human resources are key resources to be provided and exchanged. In addition to funding, the Franchisee must know what other supports the Governing Unit will provide and what the Governing Unit expects in return. In the event of unexpected changes at the community level, contingencies must also be defined and agreed upon.
- Information Systems: The Governing Unit and Franchisee must define what information they need from each other so that all parties receive the information they require to be effective and the Governing Unit receives "early warning

indications" when future dialogue or intervention may be necessary. In most cases, this involves reporting of how many people are helped and money spent.

- Rewards: In addition to the challenge of accountability, there must also be a clear definition of success and clarity about rewards that can be expected. This includes team and individual recognition.

4. Conglomerate Model

A conglomerate brings organizations together in a CCP without organizations having to give up any identity or authority. It is a close partnership without amalgamation. In this case the Governing Unit consists of representatives of each organization, but the power to make decisions remains in each organization. This model pays more attention to the boundaries of each organization.

- *Equal partnership at governance level*
- *Common vision, values and problem-definition*
- *Commonly agreed upon decision-making and accountability processes, but decision-making remains within each organization. All major decisions made by the Governing Unit must be ratified within each organization before they are finalized at the Partnership Governing Unit.*
- *Complementary roles (each party has unique strengths and resources that complement the others.)*
- *Synergies can be encouraged between organizations at various level*
- *Project functions are delivered in parallel*

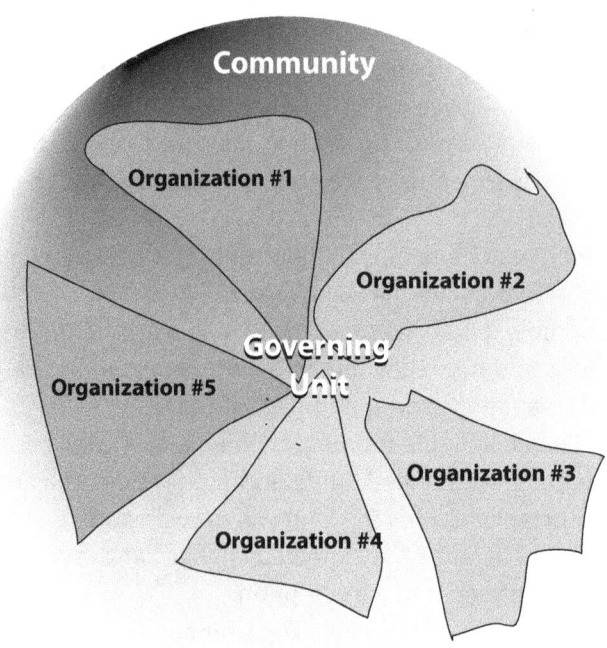

These models are ideal types. In reality, organizations may wish to choose elements from different ones to match their situation, history and circumstances.

Coalescence Spectrum: Six Levels of Autonomy and Interdependence

Definition: There are six levels to which organizations join forces, from *Networking* to *Cooperation* to *Co-ordination* to *Collective* to *Collaboration* to *Integration*[3]. Different partners may have different levels of commitment, which is reflected in the level to which they join forces or coalesce. Organizations may unite in structure and functions in different levels, regardless of whatever model of partnership they use.

Rules of Engagement: To allow movement, it is vital to define ways in which organizations and their departments can come and go, participating at various times in the project. For example, an organization may have to withdraw within two or three years or as a result of a triggering event (e.g.. funding stops or a leader moves on). This calls for defining length of term for regular reviews, change in membership status, exit clauses, and entrance criteria to allow new members to join or existing members to leave. People and organizations are allowed to change their involvement without losing face. Change in nature of involvement becomes natural and acceptable to all members.

Again, these are only examples. In reality, Partnerships take components from each level and type depending on the function, situation and nature of the organizations. For example, the Program department may be involved in an integrated fashion with other organizations in the Partnership, whereas the Human Resources department may be at a Network level.

Six Levels of Coalescence

Network
- Dialogue, clearinghouse for information
- Creates common base of support
- Loosely defined roles, connection informally based on relationships of leaders
- Low-key, minimal decision-making as a group
- Informal communication

Alliance
- Cooperation in areas needing support; limited duplication of services
- Some common role definition; ensures that tasks are done as agreed
- Joint fundraising for certain projects
- Each partner retains its own decision-making authority, identity, autonomy and responsibility for its own actions. Agreement on high-level joint decision-making.
- Decision-making need not be coordinated, as groups may decide to go on doing things differently

Coordinating Council
- Share resources to address common issues
- Merge base of resources to create new project and/or capabilities
- Central body of decision-makers
- Common and individual roles and time defined
- Formal, written agreements defining contributions, roles and responsibilities, deliverables, and milestones
- Joint budget, action plan, implementation and accountability
- Leaders are autonomous but focus together on central issue and needs

Collective
- Share resources including staff and systems to address common issues (e.g., staff secondments)
- Formalized agreement; minimum of three years commitment to shared ends
- Shared leadership; group decision-making with all partners; formalized and coordinated; some autonomy and decision-making authority is shared.
- Communication is frequent, common and high priority

Collaboration
- Formal; minimum of three years; specific roles and responsibilities for each agency
- Each partner is accountable to the other(s); use of departmental/organizational links and formal agreements
- High trust and involvement of leadership; joint decision-making including joint policies; formalized and coordinated; more autonomy and decision-making authority is assumed by the Governing Unit.
- Extensive and regular communication among leaders, department heads and organizations

Integration
- Formal merger; long-term; high intensity; organizations or members combine to create a newly structured organization which may become a legal body.
- Organizations are not only accountable to each other, there is a shared accountability and evaluation – as one body.
- They operate according to shared regulations and policies specific to the integrative agreement
- The Governing Unit has its own autonomy
- Policy and decisions re implementation are performed by the new Governing Unit in the new common structure; agreement is achieved by way of consensus or a vote.

Level of Coalescence

High level of autonomy for each organization; less joint decision-making

Low level of autonomy for each organization; more interdependence and joint decision-making

Factors to Consider When Deciding the Structure and Optimal Level of Autonomy and Interdependence:

- Number and nature of tasks to be completed
- Level of involvement of funder. Some organizations and funding agencies prefer the funder to be at the decision-making table, while some do not.
- Circumstances can necessitate, facilitate or hinder involvement on the part of the funder. Level of decision-making authority that each agency is willing to give up must be considered.
- How much coordination is required to succeed?
- Would it be best for the level of coordination to increase or decrease over time?
- Time constraints

Coalescence Checklist – Diagnostic and Developmental Tool

	Autonomy of Each Organization	Nature of Decision-making	Sharing of resources	Co-ordination of programs and services	Merging of organizations	Requires a Project Manager
Network	Highest	Separate	Lowest	Lowest	Lowest	Yes
Alliance	High	Separate	Low	Low	Low	Yes
Co-ordinating Council	Medium	Shared oversight, some operations	Some	Medium	Medium	Yes
Collective	Medium	Shared oversight and operations	Medium	Medium	Medium	Yes
Collaboration	Low	Joint	High	High	High	Yes
Integration	Lowest	Merged	Highest	Highest	Highest	Yes

This table can be used to assess how each organization sees itself and how the organizations decide to work together in a Partnership. It also spells out the movement that can be made by one or all of the organizations at different times under different conditions. Some departments within an organization can also be at different levels. Governing Unit, leaders, departments, and organizations must ask themselves these types of questions:

- **Motivation**: Why do we want to be in the Partnership?
- **Role:** What role should we play at this point in our history?
- **Type of Partnership:** How do we as a Partnership see ourselves working together, including governing ourselves, decision-making and resourcing the Partnership over time?
- **Organizational Buy-In:** How much are we prepared to give to the Partnership so that *its* needs are met? If the leader of an organization sits as a Director on the Governing Unit of the Partnership, he or she must be prepared to act in the best interests of the Partnership while in that role, even if it involves some sacrifice to some aspect of his or her organization in order to achieve the greater good and realize the vision of the Partnership.

- **Autonomy**: How much authority and freedom do the partners want to retain for their organizations?
- **Contribution of Resources:** How much are we prepared to give to the Partnership?
- **Partnership Decision-Making:** How does the Partnership want to make decisions?

The level of membership and rules of engagement should be clearly outlined in the MOU.

Memorandum of Understanding (MOU)

Each partnering organization has its unique strengths, which when synergized will leverage resources and bring about win-win situations for all.

If partners develop a realistic approach, they will be able to spearhead a coordinated initiative for community, region or country. This will require a detailed, practical, effective and feasible approach to joint governance, planning, decision-making, communication, human resources, training, financial management and accountability processes.

The many tasks that need to be undertaken must be broken down in specific fashion. All of the participating organizations will have to clarify in detail "who does what", and then determine the ingredients needed. Funding expectations must be realistic. The level of membership and engagement in the Partnership and ways of adjusting the level must also be defined in the MOU.

MOU's will need to clarify Terms of Reference further. If these prerequisites are met, the Comprehensive Community Project can become a reality.

(See Appendix – Sample MOU)

Partnership Scale

Sample[5]: (4 out of 40 questions – See Appendix for full scale)

Factor	Statement	Strongly Disagree	Disagree	No opinion	Agree	Strongly Agree
History of collaboration or cooperation in the community	1. Agencies in our community have a history of working together.					
History of collaboration or cooperation in the community	2. Trying to solve problems through collaboration has been common in this community. It's been done a lot before.					
Collaborative group seen as a legitimate leader in the community	3. Leaders in this community who are not part of our collaborative group seem hopeful about what we can accomplish.					
Collaborative group seen as a legitimate leader in the community	4. Others (in this community) who are not a part of this collaboration would generally agree that the organizations involved in this collaborative project are the "right" organizations to be effective in this new initiative.					

Roadmap: An Overall Process for Decision-Making, Quality Affirmation, Supervision and Implementation

Once the Partners have agreed to a structure and level of coalescence, they can go on to the question of how they will plan, implement and evaluate their CCP. A Roadmap describes a prototype for this overall process. This section will provide a step-by-step process for developing and operating in partnership.

Process: Normally, process is seen as a means for change. The Roadmap drives projects, defines action for all participants and delivers outcomes.

Roadmap: The Roadmap is a comprehensive planning and implementation framework. It lays out a method for organizing discussion, decision-making and project management. (See further details in Appendix.) This Roadmap oversimplifies the actual process. Nevertheless, it provides a recipe that can be adapted for most situations.

There are five key action stages in this model:
   1. Define Vision and Scope
   2. Build Partnerships
   3. Blueprint the Future
   4. Implement
   5. Learning and Improvement.

The first three phases involve a certain amount of "Muddling About", which is messy and sometimes unpredictable. These phases involve mostly right-brain thinking, which is creative, emotional, and process-oriented. For people who prefer working under a systematic plan, these phases may feel uncertain and insecure, and it may seem at times that everyone is going in circles. But this type of muddling about is vital for the various stakeholders in all levels of each organization to identify barriers that prevent them from proceeding. Solutions to those barriers can then be discussed and included in the implementation, to ensure the effectiveness of the project. These three phases involve an iterative dialogue, negotiation and decision-making process. In so doing, participants tussle about until they can build upon each other's solutions, discover common answers and agree to an action plan that they will commit to performing. This process allows all to feel heard and ensures that everyone buys into the premises that underlie the blueprint for the future.

Once the "Muddling About" is completed, and everyone agrees on the milestones and deliverables, they can "Go Forward." The two remaining phases – Implement, and Learning and Improvement – involve more left-brain thinking, which is analytical, sequential and action-oriented. The Implement phase provides 'marching orders' so that all parties can proceed in an efficient manner. This leads to a greater sense of confidence, certainty and security. These last two phases provide a more predictable and systematic approach for everyone. (See Appendix for full-size, high-res version.)

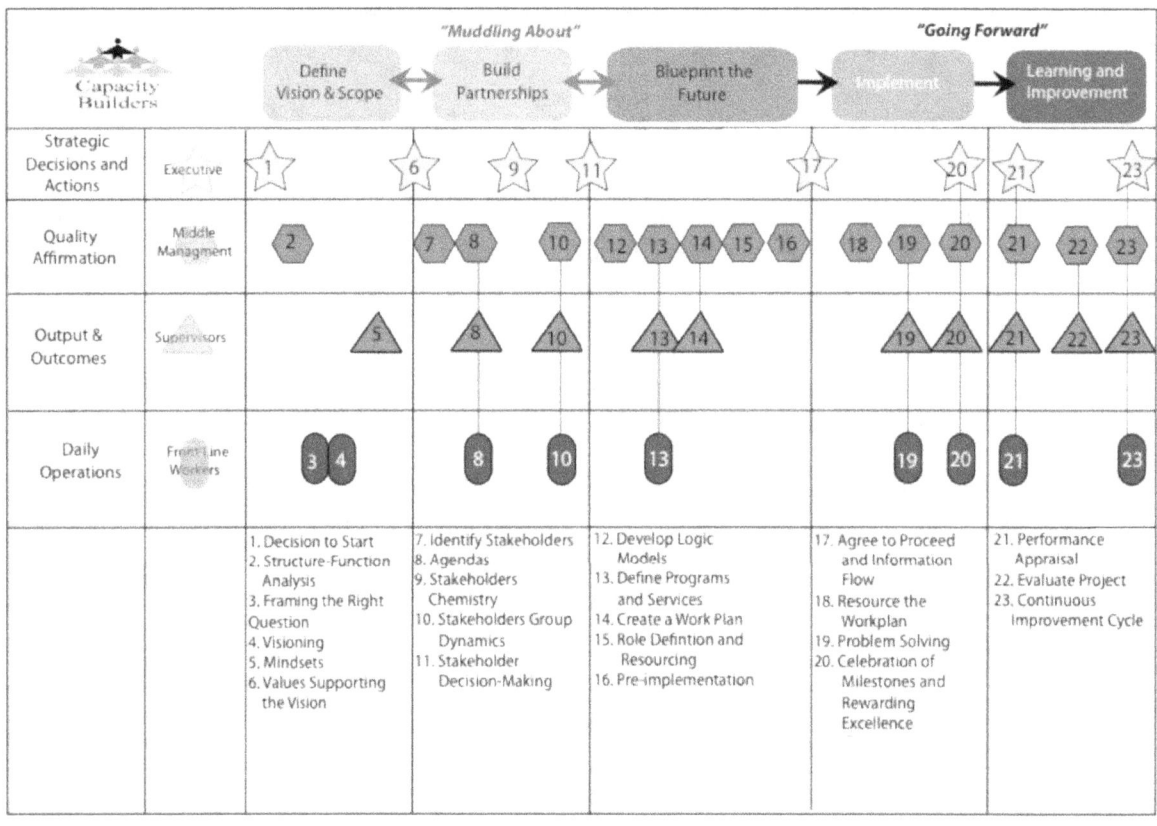

If all the key decisions are made at the top level without the engagement of middle management and front line staff, the project will not be informed by the details that will ensure it is a success. Buy-in is necessary at all levels. This graphic helps to show how the different levels of an organization interact to make decisions.

A. Define Vision and Scope: Project initiation. This stage determines the vision and scope of the project. **It is important that partners work on the following steps together:**

1. Decision to Start: How did things develop and how are they operating now? This decision is usually based on a consensus on the vision and overall outcome of the project (start with the end in mind). It also involves settling the overall scope or boundaries of the project, including the extent of activities, target population, geography and length of time it will occur.

2. Structure-Functional Analysis: Who is doing what now? What functions are each stakeholder handling currently and what needs to change in order to define and address the problem?

3. Framing the Right Question: What is the impact and challenge you are seeking to address? It is important to identify the right goals and issues; otherwise the results and solutions will be off-target. 80% of the solution is how you define the question or problem.

4. Visioning: This stage involves agreeing on what the new reality could be. The scope needs to be feasible – not too big yet not too small. It also requires emotional and financial buy-in to the new reality by all stakeholders. The right-sized dream or promise is key to having the most suitable vision. Settling on the right scope requires that the stakeholders work through the process in a creative fashion together. If the scope is to be realistic, the partners must come up with the appropriate resources. For example, if the stakeholders are dreaming of a national scope but only have sufficient resources for a village, it cannot be realized during that time period.

5. Mindsets: What paradigms have kept the current situation in place? What new worldviews and assumptions must be adopted to support the intended change based on the problem definition?

6. Values supporting the vision: Identify the criteria that have been agreed upon by stakeholders, and that will be used to justify and evaluate decisions within the realm of the new vision e.g., honesty, integrity, charity.

B. Build Partnerships: This stage will enable participating stakeholders to determine what type of partnership model is needed

7. Identify stakeholders: Who are your stakeholders? Who really needs to be at the table at each stage of the project for the vision to be realized?

8. Agendas: What are the stated agendas versus the unstated agendas for the leaders and their organizations? The leaders must initiate this process, but because it is one of the most critical stages in the building of a project, all levels of the organization must acknowledge and contribute. See 'The Element Questions' in appendix.

9. Stakeholder Chemistry: What is the nature of the relationships between the leaders of the stakeholder groups?

10. Stakeholder Group Dynamics: stages of the Partnership and sub-groups e.g. forming, norming, storming and performing.

11. Stakeholder Decision-making: Who will play what role in decision-making within and between organizations and as a Partnership?

C. Blueprint the Future: This stage determines the roles and responsibilities, deliverables and action plan, and creates a safe environment for change.

12. Develop Logic Models: Articulate and explain how outcomes will be achieved through programs and services over the short, medium and long term phases of the project.

13. Define Programs and Services: What services, programs and products are going to be carried out?

14. Create a Work Plan: What steps are involved in developing and carrying out the programs and services at all levels? What does the literature say are the best practices for each major component of your programs and services? What needs to be done at what time? Identify milestones and resources.

15. Role Definition and Resourcing: Define roles, authorities, responsibilities, resources, training and equipment. Also determine how to monitor support and provide accountability.

16. Pre-Implementation: Before a plan can be implemented, all parties must work out appropriate procedures, policies and agreements that address their own concerns and the inter-organizational dynamics that will evolve when the organizations start working together. This phase also addresses funders concerns to ensure accountability.

D. Implement: This stage defines the key steps and processes for implementing the plan.

17. Agree to Proceed and Ensure Flow of Information: Information flow must include reporting and accountability.

17. Resource the Workplan: Ensure that you have the right people with the right knowledge and skills in the right jobs.

 18. Problem-solving: Problems occur at all levels and therefore also are defined and solved at all levels, depending on the authority and the scope of project roles. Where possible, delegate problem solving and authority as close to the ground level as possible, commensurate with responsibility.

19. Celebration of Milestones and Rewarding Excellence: How do we know when a milestone is reached? How do we reward excellence?

NOTE: identify key information for each level, including roles of Executive, Middle Management, Supervisors and Frontline Workers.

5. Learning and Improvement: In addition to defining the project assessment criteria, ongoing learning defines how all of the partners will assess themselves and how they will improve as they go forward.

20. Performance Appraisal: Are all the project departments and personnel performing as efficiently and effectively as possible?

21. Evaluate Project: Did the project achieve the short and midterm outcomes? Were they on time? Were they on budget?

22. Continuous Improvement Cycle: How will everyone learn and improve with time? How will these learnings be incorporated into future practice and forward planning?

Conclusion

In order to realize the dreams of the Comprehensive Community Project, each stakeholder and the group must expand their range of thinking and collaborative working methods. Comprehensive Community Project planning gives them a framework to bring many parties together to reach goals beyond our separate capabilities. *"None of us is as smart or as capable as all of us."* Currently, no one party has the mandate, resources or ability to address a community-wide, nationwide or regional challenge. The synergy among individuals and organizations is essential to achieve the ends of the Comprehensive Community Project.

About the Authors

Bill Locke is the founder of Capacity Builders, a Calgary-based consulting company that has provided strategic development services to over 200 community organizations, foundations and government departments around the world. He has played an instrumental role in creating and leading numerous comprehensive community projects in the past 30 years. He and his wife Laura have three grown children.

Dr. Christie has over 40 years of direct senior and executive management experience and specializes in the development of organizations and the management of strategic change in human service organizations. He has a Masters degree focusing on community development and a Doctorate in the field of managing strategic change in complex organizations. He and his wife Mavis live in Calgary, Alberta.

Other Capacity Builders Publications

The Nurturing Leader: A Toolkit for Every Season of Organizational Growth (2010) by Bill Locke and Joel Christie, PhD

Contact Info

For further assistance, contact:
Bill Locke, President, Capacity Builders
(403) 874-1814 (cell)
(403) 284-2863 (fax)
www.capacitybuilders.org

Bibliography

[1] David O. Renz "An Overview of Nonprofit Governance", adapted from a chapter prepared for Philanthropy in America: A Comprehensive Historical Encyclopedia, (2004), Dwight Burlingame, ed.

[2] David O. Renz "An Overview of Nonprofit Governance", adapted from a chapter prepared for Philanthropy in America: A Comprehensive Historical Encyclopedia, (2004), Dwight Burlingame, ed.

[3] Bergstrom, Arno et al. (1995). Collaboration Framework—Addressing Community Capacity. National Network for Collaboration.

[4] The Nurturing Leader: A Toolkit for Every Season of Organizational Growth (2010) Locke and Christie

[5] Adapted from Wilder Collaboration Inventory (see full version in Appendix)

[6] Imaginization: New Mindsets for Seeing, Organizing and Managing, Gareth Morgan (1997)

- <u>The Nurturing Leader: A Toolkit for Every Season of Organizational Growth</u> (2010) by Bill Locke and Joel Christie, PhD
- Elements questions and analysis
- Wilder Collaboration Factors Inventory – 40 Questions
- Sample MOU between NPO's: "CCP Partnership MOU TEMPLATE.doc"
- CCP Governing Unit Terms of Reference
- Partnership Rating Chart
- Partnership Agreement Tool
- Roadmap

The Nurturing Leader

A Toolkit for Every Season of Organizational Growth

Bill Locke
Joel Christie, PhD

Table of Contents

Element:
What external drivers are important to this element?

1) What are the values and assumptions on which this element is based?

What organizational culture would support and realize these values?

2) What are the services and programs in this element?

Who will do what?

Define the organizational structures needed to support these programs and services.

Define the processes and communication required to deliver each program and service.

3) How will decisions be made and resources allocated?
Who will be able to decide what?

Define the enabling structure required:
- Internally:
- Externally:

Define the enabling processes required:
- Internally:
- Externally:

What are the accountability processes for each service and program?

The Wilder Collaboration Factors Inventory

| Name of Collaboration Project | Date |

Statements about Your Collaborative Group:

Factor	Statement	Strongly Disagree	Disagree	Neutral, No Opinion	Agree	Strongly Agree
History of collaboration or cooperation in the community	1. Agencies in our community have a history of working together	1	2	3	4	5
	2. Trying to solve problems through collaboration has been common in this community. It's been done a lot before.	1	2	3	4	5
Collaborative group seen as a legitimate leader in the community	3. Leaders in this community who are not part of our collaborative group seem hopeful about what we can accomplish.	1	2	3	4	5
	4. Others (in this community) who are not a part of this collaboration would generally agree that the organizations involved in this collaborative project are the "right" organizations to make this work.	1	2	3	4	5
Favorable political and social climate	5. The political and social climate seems to be "right" for starting a collaborative project like this one.	1	2	3	4	5
	6. The time is right for this collaborative project.	1	2	3	4	5
Mutual respect, understanding, and trust	7. People involved in our collaboration always trust one another.	1	2	3	4	5
	8. I have a lot of respect for the other people involved in this collaboration.	1	2	3	4	5
Appropriate cross section of members	9. The people involved in our collaboration represent a cross section of those who have a stake in what we are trying to accomplish.	1	2	3	4	5
	10. All the organizations that we need to be members of this collaborative group have become members of the group.	1	2	3	4	5
Members see collaboration as in their self-interest	11. My organization will benefit from being involved in this collaboration.	1	2	3	4	5
Ability to compromise	12. People involved in our collaboration are willing to compromise on important aspects of our project.	1	2	3	4	5
Members share a stake in both process and outcome	13. The organizations that belong to our collaborative group invest the right amount of time in our collaborative efforts.	1	2	3	4	5

Factor	Statement	Strongly Disagree	Disagree	Neutral, No Opinion	Agree	Strongly Agree
	14. Everyone who is a member of our collaborative group wants this project to succeed.	1	2	3	4	5
	15. The level of commitment among the collaboration participants is high.	1	2	3	4	5
Multiple layers of participation	16. When the collaborative group makes major decisions, there is always enough time for members to take information back to their organizations to confer with colleagues about what the decision should be.	1	2	3	4	5
	17. Each of the people who participate in decisions in this collaborative group can speak for the entire organization they represent, not just a part.	1	2	3	4	5
Flexibility	18. There is a lot of flexibility when decisions are made; people are open to discussing different options.	1	2	3	4	5
	19. People in this collaborative group are open to different approaches to how we can do our work. They are willing to consider different ways of working.	1	2	3	4	5
Development of clear roles and policy guidelines	20. People in this collaborative group have a clear sense of their roles and responsibilities.	1	2	3	4	5
	21. There is a clear process for making decisions among the partners in this collaboration.	1	2	3	4	5
Adaptability	22. This collaboration is able to adapt to changing conditions, such as fewer funds than expected, changing political climate, or change in leadership.	1	2	3	4	5
	23. This group has the ability to survive even if it had to make major changes in its plans or add some new members in order to reach its goals.	1	2	3	4	5
Appropriate pace of development	24. This collaborative group has tried to take on the right amount of work at the right pace.	1	2	3	4	5
	25. We are currently able to keep up with the work necessary to coordinate all the people, organizations, and activities related to this collaborative project.	1	2	3	4	5
Open and frequent communication	26. People in this collaboration communicate openly with one another.	1	2	3	4	5

Factor	Statement	Strongly Disagree	Disagree	Neutral, No Opinion	Agree	Strongly Agree
	27. I am informed as often as I should be about what goes on in the collaboration.	1	2	3	4	5
	28. The people who lead this collaborative group communicate well with the members.	1	2	3	4	5
Established informal relationships and communication links	29. Communication among the people in this collaborative group happens both at formal meetings and in informal ways.	1	2	3	4	5
	30. I personally have informal conversations about the project with others who are involved in this collaborative group.	1	2	3	4	5
Concrete, attainable goals and objectives	31. I have a clear understanding of what our collaboration is trying to accomplish.	1	2	3	4	5
	32. People in our collaborative group know and understand our goals.	1	2	3	4	5
	33. People in our collaborative group have established reasonable goals.	1	2	3	4	5
Shared vision	34. The people in this collaborative group are dedicated to the idea that we can make this project work.	1	2	3	4	5
	35. My ideas about what we want to accomplish with this collaboration seem to be the same as the ideas of others.	1	2	3	4	5
Unique purpose	36. What we are trying to accomplish with our collaborative project would be difficult for any single organization to accomplish by itself.	1	2	3	4	5
	37. No other organization in the community is trying to do exactly what we are trying to do.	1	2	3	4	5
Sufficient funds, staff, materials, and time	38. Our collaborative group had adequate funds to do what it wants to accomplish.	1	2	3	4	5
	39. Our collaborative group has adequate "people power" to do what it wants to accomplish.	1	2	3	4	5
Skilled leadership	40. The people in leadership positions for this collaboration have good skills for working with other people and organizations.	1	2	3	4	5

Memorandum of Understanding

Between
Organization A
Organization B
Organization C
Organization D
Organization E

---

1.   Understanding

Organization A; Organization B; Organization C; Organization D and Organization E ("The Partners") are pleased to enter into this Memorandum of Understanding to collectively govern, plan, implement and evaluate the Comprehensive Plan ("CCP"). This Understanding may be renewed upon successful completion of the three-year pilot and may be revised to include other Partners over time.

This Understanding sets out the objectives, commitments, responsibilities, and activities of the Partnership. This document is written for the purpose of confirming understandings between The Partners and the administrative fiscal agent. The administrative fiscal agent is considered to be a member of The Partners for the purposes of this Understanding. This is not a legally binding document.

2.   Duration

This agreement will extend from _____ to _____. (Minimum of <u>Three</u> Years)

3.   Objectives of the Partnership

The Partners have entered into the Partnership to form a decision-making and implementation structure for CCP. The Partners will make collective decisions about the governance, planning, implementation and evaluation of CCP.

Decisions will reflect agreement among The Partners about the outcomes that they seek to achieve through their joint efforts and contributions; the purposes for which and ways in which their efforts and contributions may be realized; and the ways in which the CCP and CCP programs will be required to demonstrate accountability to the funding sources.

The Partners, along with the CCP Project Manager will serve as the Governing Unit for CCP. The terms of reference for the Governing Unit as set out in Schedule A form part of this Understanding.

4.   Efforts and Contributions

Each signatory to this Understanding (with the exception of the fiscal agent) will contribute efforts and contributions to CCP on an annual basis. The amount of efforts and contributions made by each partner may vary from year to year. However, the partners will collectively strive to ensure that the total amount of efforts and contributions made in the first year of the pilot does not decrease in the second or third year of the pilot.

The efforts and contributions made by each partner will be pooled and distributed under the Governing Unit.

This Memorandum of Understanding does not supersede or in any way affect any pre-existing agreements between any of The Partners.

Each partner must obtain approval from the other partners before formally soliciting new efforts and contributions for CCP.

5.   Structure

One person will be selected to represent each of the partners for the duration of the pilot. Each partner may assign staff support as required to support their effective involvement in the Partnership.

6.   Decision-Making

The Governing Unit will make decisions by a) concensus or b) majority vote or c) 75% majority vote or d) 100% agreement by Partners impacted by the decision.

7.   Project Manager

A Project Manager will report to the Governing Unit. The Project Manager will be responsible for the co-ordination, implementation and evaluation of the programs as directed by the Governing Unit.

8.   Operating Processes

The Partners will develop and commit to a unified system for planning and priority setting, and for establishing program criteria, program allocations, and reporting/accountability requirements.

The Partners and any other invited partners will collectively determine which programs will receive efforts and contributions.

All programs will be coordinated through the Project Manager.

9.   Media and Public Relations

No material from the Committee will be made available to people outside the Committee without prior approval by the Committee members.

All funding partners must be acknowledged in any communications about CCP with the media or the public.

Any media attention about CCP solicited by one or more of the funding partners or by CCP administration must be approved by all the funding partners.

9.   Withdrawals from and Additions to Membership

Any signatory to this Memorandum of Understanding may withdraw from the agreement upon 60 days' written notice to the other signatories, provided that contributions have been made as per the partner's agreed-upon contributions to the funding pool and will not be withdrawn from the funding pool.

Additional Partners may be admitted as partners as determined by The Partners. New partners must agree to the conditions as set out in this Understanding and be signatories to the Understanding.

10.   Confidentiality

Representatives of The Partners shall not divulge personal or confidential information revealed to them by reason of their participation in the Partnership.

11.   Conflict of Interest

No member of this Committee shall personally benefit in any way from his or her involvement in the Partnership.

IN FULL UNDERSTANDING OF THE TERMS OF THIS MEMORANDUM OF UNDERSTANDING, THE PARTNERSHAVE HERETO SET THEIR HAND.

for the Organization A:

_____	_____	_____
Name	Title	Date

for the Organization B:

_____	_____	_____
Name	Title	Date

for Organization C:

_____	_____	_____
Name	Title	Date

for Organization D:

_____	_____	_____
Name	Title	Date

for the Organization E:

_____	_____	_____
Name	Title	Date

CCP

Governing Unit
Terms of Reference

1. Governing Unit Purpose

The Governing Unit is responsible for the financial and evaluation oversight of the Comprehensive Plan.

The Governing Unit will:
- Support the Steering Committee to oversee the execution of the vision and mission for the project, although the Organization E, acting as the Fiscal Agent for all administrative operations, will oversee day-to-day administrative operations;
- Serve as the decision-making body for project funding and budget, evaluation and structure of the project;
- Support and provide guidance to the staff and fiscal agent of the project; and
- Promote comprehensive strategies, plan collaborative approaches and ensure the project moves forward smoothly.

2. Project Description

In May of 2006 the project Partners (Organization A; Organization B; Organization C; Organization D and Organization E) and agencies involved with the mandate started to work together to design the Comprehensive Plan. They designed a structure to enhance and coordinate the program and services in the communities of X, Y and Z. These communities were selected based on a number of criteria including readiness of the communities, clients living within the community they live and the variety of service providers currently offering programs locally. This project will allow us to build on the strengths within the communities.

The **vision** is for clients with the stated populations, thus providing positive opportunities for engagement within their communities.

To accomplish this vision, the **mission** is to create a comprehensive network of high quality programs that promote positive development for all clients in the targeted communities.

3. Project Timeline

This demonstration project is planned for 2007 – 2010 and will be evaluated with the intention of bringing the successful components to other areas of the region.

4. Governing Unit Membership

The Governing Unit will be composed of management-level representatives of the funding organizations and the fiscal agent of the project. The Project Manager will coordinate the Governing Unit meetings. The project evaluator will report to the Governing Unit and attend meetings as required.

5. **Key Duties and Responsibilities of the** Governing Unit

The key duty of the Governing Unit members will be to provide guidance, advice, and assistance to the CCP project staff and, specifically, to:
- Regularly attend Governing Unit meetings. Members who are unable to attend a given meeting are responsible to provide input in advance of the meeting so that those members who are present can make decisions that reflect diverse views and comply with the project timelines;
- Review documentation, provide feedback and guidance to the project staff and the project evaluator, and participate in decisions regarding proposed approaches and tools;
- Provide any documentation and information that is relevant to the project objectives;
- Review and provide feedback on the draft(s) of each report prepared by the project staff and the project evaluator within one week of submission;
- Bring knowledge and feedback from Governing Unit meetings to other committees and networks relating to after school hours programming;
- Promote CCP among peers, colleagues, and the community; and
- Liaise with the Organization E as required, which is serving as fiscal agent to the project.

6. **Accountability**

- The Fiscal Agent, or its designate, will be responsible for completing any financial reports for CCP.
- The Fiscal Agent of the project is accountable to the Governing Unit for project funds. Project staff is accountable to the Fiscal Agent.
- The Governing Unit will liaise with the CCP Steering Committee with respect to completing any reports for the project.
- The Governing Unit is responsible for securing funding for the project.

7. **Decision-making**

The decisions of the Governing Unit will be made by consensus. If for whatever reason, consensus cannot be achieved, the Committee may agree to an alternative process, such as voting. Deliberations will remain confidential unless there is general agreement and consensus to make them public.

It is recognized that these decisions will not be binding on any members of the Committee unless and until the governing bodies of their respective organizations have approved them.

8. **Meeting schedule**

The Governing Unit will convene at least four times each fiscal year.

9. **Invited Guests**

The Governing Unit may, from time to time, invite other stakeholders or representatives to attend meetings as presenters, advisers, or observers.
-

The Partnership Rating Chart

The Partnership Rating Chart was prepared by the Collaboration Roundtable Spring 2001, BC Ministry of Community Development. It gives an overview of the readiness, strengths and challenges that each partner brings to the CCP. This table also can be used to help define the complementary roles and functions the various partners fulfill as they progress through the "Road Map".

Partnership Rating Chart

Each element identified below is explained in the following pages.

ELEMENTS Rate each partner on a scale of 1-5 on the following elements	PARTNER A	PARTNER B	PARTNER C
1. Has similar organizational culture			
2. Is cultural sensitive			
3. Values acceptance and integration			
4. Has a solid reputation			
5. Shares your vision			
6. Has common goals and objectives			
7. Has clear division of roles and responsibilities			
8. Has skills and capacity you need			
9. Communicates effectively			
10. Has effective ways of resolving conflicts			
11. Is flexible and adaptable			
12. Has a supportive leadership style			
13. Recognizes and rewards success			
14. Willing to share decision-making authority; willing to give up some autonomy			
15. Has similar accountability processes			
16. Has similar administrative processes			
17. Has similar wages and benefits structure			
18. Has procedures to deal with liability issues			
19. Willing to share resources			
20. Willing to have a partnership agreement			
21. Shows commitment			
22. Willing to reassess the partnership			
23. Provides added value			
24. Fosters a sense of trust			
TOTALS			

Partnership Agreement Tool

(Based on the WWF-UK Organizational Development Unit toolkit)

1 Vision

What is the vision for the partnership?

2 Quality

Is there a commitment to improving the quality of the relationship over time? Is the quality of service integral in all organizations connected to your agreement?

3 Educational objectives

How will the partnership contribute to organizations' fulfilling their mandates? What are your agreed activities, goals and outcomes? Have you identified areas of potential or actual service collaboration?
Will outcomes:
- support mutual respect between clients
- challenge and inform perceptions of development issues
- develop critical thinking
- encourage open-mindedness
- develop participatory skills?

4 Values and principles

What are organizations' values and principles? How do these complement each other? Are there any non-negotiable expectations concerning values and principles?

5 Mutual trust and respect

How can mutual trust and respect be established? How will a breakdown of trust and/or respect be dealt with?

6 Sustainability

How integral is the partnership to the organizations involved? What resources (people, time, skills, finance, external support) are needed to sustain the partnership? How might community involvement make the partnerships more sustainable?

7 Inclusiveness and equality

How inclusive is the partnership? How can marginalized individuals and groups (in organization and local communities) be more involved? What can be done to ensure that the partnership is based on equality?

8 Obligations and responsibilities

What roles and responsibilities does each organization have? What rights and obligations does each organization have?

9   Reporting, reviewing and reflection

What frameworks will be used for reporting, reviewing and reflection? What will be done to ensure that this is a two-way and on-going process?

10   Monitoring and evaluation

How will progress be measured, including the development of the partnership itself? What will be done to ensure that this is an open and collaborative process? What will be the indicators for success? Who will determine these?

11   Timelines

Are there indicative and actual timelines related to specific tasks and outcomes?   How necessary are these?

12   Financial issues

If money is involved, what are the terms, conditions, accounting standards, accountability, etc?

13   Fund-raising

If fund-raising happens, are there procedures to ensure the equal participation of all partners in planning, undertaking fund-raising activities and in agreeing on the use of funds raised? Are financial and other contributions valued equally?

14   Conflict resolution

What mechanisms will be used to resolve conflicts? What role might third parties play (if any)?

Capacity Builders

"Muddling About" → "Going Forward"

Phases: Define Vision & Scope — Build Partnerships — Blueprint the Future — Learning and Improvement

Capacity Builders		Define Vision & Scope	Build Partnerships	Blueprint the Future	Learning and Improvement
Strategic Decisions and Actions	Executive	1	6 9 11	17	21 23
Quality Affirmation	Middle Managment	2	7 8 10	12 13 14 15 16 18 19 20	21 22 23
Output & Outcomes	Supervisors	5	8 10	13 14	19 20 21 22 23
Daily Operations	Front Line Workers	3 4	8 10	13	19 20 21 23

1. Decision to Start
2. Structure-Function Analysis
3. Framing the Right Question
4. Visioning
5. Mindsets
6. Values Supporting the Vision

7. Identify Stakeholders
8. Agendas
9. Stakeholders Chemistry
10. Stakeholders Group Dynamics
11. Stakeholder Decision-Making

12. Develop Logic Models
13. Define Programs and Services
14. Create a Work Plan
15. Role Defintion and Resourcing
16. Pre-implementation

17. Agree to Proceed and Information Flow
18. Resource the Workplan
19. Problem Solving
20. Celebration of Milestones and Rewarding Excellence

21. Performance Appraisal
22. Evaluate Project
23. Continuous Improvement Cycle

www.ingramcontent.com/pod-product-compliance
Lightning Source LLC
Chambersburg PA
CBHW080109010626
45794CB00015B/3339